TIPS FOR TEENS

Telephone Tactics, Petting Practices, and
Other Milestones on the Road to Popularity

Benjamin Darling

CHRONICLE BOOKS
SAN FRANCISCO

Library of Congress Cataloging-in-Publication Data:

Darling, Benjamin, 1966-
    Tips for teens: telephone tactics, petting practices, and other
milestones on the road to popularity / Benjamin Darling.
        p.   cm.
    ISBN 0-8118-0520-4
    1. Teenagers—United States—Life skills guides—Humor.
    2. Etiquette for children and teenagers—Humor. I. Title.
    HQ796.D26 1994
    305.23'5—dc20   93—35815
                                                                      CIP

Printed in Hong Kong.

Book and Cover Design: Palomine Design Studio

Distributed in Canada by Raincoast Books,
112 East Third Avenue, Vancouver, B.C. V5T 1C8

10 9 8 7 6 5 4 3 2 1

Chronicle Books
275 Fifth Street
San Francisco, CA 94103

TIPS FOR TEENS

How to be tops in your teens

During my brief sojourn in high school a disproportionate number of my valuable educational hours were spent in the school office waiting admittance to the principal's chamber. I sat in a rather uncomfortable orange plastic chair with my head resting against the bulletin board. From this vantage point, I had ample opportunity to observe the school secretary, and it is of this sterling woman that I wish to speak.

Though I do not remember her name I am sure it ended in a *y*, perhaps Cathy (with a *C*) or Jenny or Becky. I remember her because of her youthfulness. She was always bouncy and girlish, a sixteen-year-old trapped in an aging body. Whatever the gravity of the offense that had brought me thither she considered it to be merely a teenage prank, a bubbling over of high spirits, similar to something she and her chums might have done only last week. She would smile slyly when she read a note from one of my teachers outlining my sins, all the while wagging a finger at me as if I were merely Tom Sawyer caught stealing a bit of jam. I believe she may have even chucked me under the chin once or twice.

In the course of these frequent visits to the school office, I had many a conversation with this monument to youthful exuberance. I discovered that she had spent the majority of her life in this same high school (save for a brief hiatus to bear children and raise them to high school age); she had, for perhaps decades, rarely left its confines during school hours. She dearly wished to remain a young person forever, and staying in high school was one way to realize her dream. Although she worked for the grown-ups she considered herself one of us, part of the student body.

Indeed, our school secretary was the most enthusiastic member of our student body, participating in mandated school activities with a giddy vigor that actual teenagers, crippled by an odd mixture of apathy and desire, couldn't muster. On Halloween she was elaborately dressed as a witch, typing away happily on her Selectric and answering the telephone in a croaky witch's voice. Pep rallies and homecoming days gave her an opportunity to further indulge her already strong desire to dress in the school colors. On these days she coordinated her outfit right down to the earrings and nail polish, and if it happened to be warm that day, and she wore sandals, her toenails would be painted as well. Her shining moment was fifties day, when she would step pertly down the hall in original and perfectly maintained saddle shoes and poodle skirt (the poodle's features being annually refreshed with little bits of felt and glitter). She was her most young and beautiful on fifties day, and, if you let your eyes go slightly out of focus, she appeared no older than seventeen.

I should have appreciated her more. At the time I saw her to be an amusing anomaly along the well-trodden path to the principal's office. I saw her as a conformist in a time of rebels, little realizing that her vision was utterly unique.

It is for my school secretary—Becky, Jenny, or Cathy—that this book was created. It is a guide to that slim and delicious moment between childhood and adulthood, a time of increasing discovery and diminishing innocence, and, for some, a time that never

How Long Will a Date Wait?

existed. Now that we are older many of us are ready to regain or create anew our teenagehood; to feel the thrill of asking for a first date, to have friends to our house to listen to records and dance, to kiss in a car. We are prepared to enjoy in smaller degrees the compromising of our innocence and thereby enjoy it more fully.

I encourage the reader to use this book in the spirit my school secretary would have. —*Benjamin Darling.*

Contents

The male sex hormone brings about the
appearance of whiskers, the growth of body
hair, and the deepening of the voice.

8

The function of the female sex hormone is to cause the girl's voice to deepen a little, hair to grow on the body, and the breasts to develop, changes which occur in the process of maturation.

Right Eating . . . Keeps You Swingin'!

Did you ever sit down and seriously consider the way you eat? How much snacking? How many meals skipped or hurried? How much overly rich food . . . without enough fruits, vegetables and milk included?

Don't feel too badly if you haven't really concentrated on this . . . most of us don't. Eating is a habit, but *that's* reason enough to give your food some serious thought. For you are forming a lifetime of eating habits right now *every* day at *every* meal.

Many of us may not be wealthy nor terribly wise when we're older, but each of us does have within himself the chance to be healthy. And good health is based on a sensible three-way combination of sufficient rest, exercise and an adequate, well-balanced diet.

Nutrition may sound puzzling, but reduced to simple, everyday terms, it's mealtime habits that assure clear skin, pretty teeth, strong bones and the extra "bounce" of vitality that gives energy for work and play.

And during growing years, every teenager needs more of the important protective elements than at any other time of life. So let's think about eating, now, and for the future, shall we?

10

Everybody's Doing It . . . Eating, that is!

If you haven't already thought about it, you'll soon discover that eating is something one does with others . . . family, friends or new acquaintances at parties and school gatherings. You'll find your tastes may differ from those of others, but this will be true through a whole lifetime of eating. Consider these few hints . . . they may help you do a better job of setting your own food habits.

EAT LIKE A MEMBER OF THE FAMILY by being considerate of meals served in your home. Perhaps you *don't* care for baked squash, lamb stew or asparagus. Remember, though, your mother considers four or five tastes, the budget and her available time when she plans meals.

LEARN TO LIKE MOST FOODS. Instead of being critical when some new dish appears, give it a try! Don't automatically say, "I'm not going to like that!"

BE WISE ABOUT SNACKS. Sometimes three meals a day aren't enough. But you'll find it only makes good complexion and figure sense to snack sensibly. One can store up many hidden calories with gooey sundaes, carbonated beverages and rich deserts.

TAKE AN INTEREST IN THE KITCHEN. There's more to meals than eating, you know. Perhaps you'd like to make a few suggestions about family food. Well, *earn* that privilege with a helping hand. Do the marketing occasionally, clean up the kitchen without grumbling, and yes, even prepare a meal or two during the week. Take the responsibility for refreshments when the crowd comes to your house. Cultivate an interest in such things—because you'll be doing them in a home of your own.

11

You're *Your Own* Show!

Rest, relaxation, and good food all *help* keep a clear skin, shiny hair, good teeth and bones, but they aren't the *whole* story. Good grooming and an attractive appearance are extremely important to us at *any* age.

Let's start with posture. Think about walking tall . . . it's surprising how much better clothes look! There'll be fewer backaches, or even headaches, too. Don't slouch as you walk, nor slump as you sit. Relax! Lift your head and shoulders, then walk as if you're going *somewhere*. Sit comfortably with light at the proper angle when you study. Concentrate on posture to develop good walking and sitting habits.

Look at yourself in the mirror! Have you a regular nighttime, morning and weekly cleanliness program? Soon you'll be at college or on your own; no family to remind you of the toothbrush, nail file, comb or soap and water. Yet regular attention to teeth, nails and hair is a habit just as important to good health as food.

Give that room of yours the "once-over." Of course you meant to hang things up after last night's party, but did you *do* it? It's only smart to hang clothes in your closet immediately—they need less pressing and laundry care that way. And tidy, wrinkle-free clothing is an important part of the shined-and-polished look!

Just remember, most of us wouldn't take the first prize in a beauty contest. Yet it's possible, with some time and attention, to improve the looks we have. So form good grooming habits *now*—for the rest of your life.

A Helping Hand Along the Way

Face facts! There's no simple way through growing years. But the family doctor and dentist can be good friends. You'll learn from either of them that others your age have figure or skin problems or need some major dental repairs. Don't be foolish . . . instead of ignoring your tooth decay, following faddish diets, or worse yet, cutting out a daily meal or two when you're lumpy in spots, get sensible medical and dental assistance along the way. Then cooperate . . . *follow* the recommendations given you.

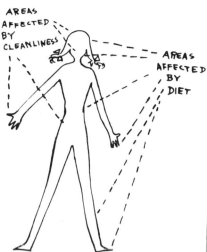

AREAS AFFECTED BY CLEANLINESS

AREAS AFFECTED BY DIET

CALORIE COUNT

In actuality, then, beauty is lots more than skin deep. Beauty is as deep as you are. Beauty is all of you, your face, your figure, your skin. More than any other part, though, your skin will be the barometer of your beauty weather. It will tell you how well you are keeping to a beauty schedule. A broken-out complexion is a sure sign that you have slipped up somewhere. It is an indication that you have eaten too many sweets or skimped on cleanliness. Remember to be diligent in your daily habits, and your reward will be a smooth, silken complexion (and, not incidentally, a fine face and figure).

First Aid for Allowances

Mr. Webster, the dictionary writer, says that an allowance is "a sum of money granted periodically to a dependent." The "dependent" is you. Don't you think you receive enough?

Count your blessings! When those Antique Adults were young, your weekly allowance might have been their spending money for a month. Yet today's dozens of creams, lotions, purses, records take money. Why not discover the big, wide world of earning some?

Don't expect to be paid for keeping your room tidy, helping around the kitchen, or planting a few petunias in the family garden. You aren't a paying guest who expects such service. You share household tasks as a part of family contribution. Become a Blue Ribbon Baby Sitter.

Blue Ribbon Baby Sitting

A baby-sitting job is no time for watching TV programs not permitted at home. You are being rewarded with money by parents who wish to enjoy some much-needed relaxation. Mothers have a remarkable way of comparing notes on sitters. If you are serious about earning a few dollars, shape up!

Arrange a definite time for sitting. Inform your family when they may expect you home. Arrive on time, or a few minutes early to check facts before parents depart. If there is no list of the following, make one up quickly:

✓ Telephone number where parents, or a responsible adult may be reached in an emergency

✓ Local Police and Fire Department telephone numbers

✓ Arrangements for feeding children and bedtime

✓ Telephone answering instructions

Act as if this is business. You are being paid. Bring a book, your homework or knitting. Don't arm yourself with a long list of telephone numbers for a four-hour gab session. Don't treat your employer's refrigerator as a free raid on the local drive-in. Don't glue your nose to TV and overlook sleeping children. Check them every half hour.

Before bed, little ones often need a bottle. No cause for panic. The wiggles, small cries and faces are baby ways of saying, "Where's my nightcap?" Be prepared a few minutes before feeding time to avoid a long hungry roar.

Once the children are bedded down, be fairly near the telephone. Light sleepers are frequently awakened by its ring. Should the phone ring, answer as your employer has directed. Be sure to write down messages. *Never* say, "This is Ann. The family is out, and I am baby-sitting with the children" to a stranger. Sad but true, this occasionally leads to harm to you or the children.

The Blue Ribbon Baby Sitter is dependable and completely aware of her responsibility for others. Expect to be out of a job if you eat four hot dogs, two bottles of chilled cola, three packs of snacks, run up the phone bill with unnecessary calls to friends, or permit boy or girl friends to join you without permission!

P.S. *You may quite properly ask one of the parents to see you safely home.*

Letter Etiquette

A letter is a piece of private property. It is considered a serious breach of good manners to open a letter addressed to another (even a member of your own family) or to read a letter you find lying about opened. Keep in mind, too, that letters are not intended for general circulation like a newspaper. The boy or girl who, for amusement or curiosity, shows a sentimental or confidential letter he or she has received reveals coarse feelings. Do not write any very personal message on a postcard. This is not considerate. A postcard is hardly more private than a poster.

Do not seal a letter that you give to a friend to deliver. If it is a letter of introduction, you will probably show it to him anyway.

Who writes the first letter when two friends separate? The one who has gone away, regardless of sex.

Telephoning comes into its own during the teen years. The instrument which was used only casually during childhood is jealously guarded by adolescents as a priceless means of communication. Dates are made and broken over it. What to wear and where to go and what to do are all discussed over it.

How to Place a Telephone Call

There is a know-how of telephoning another that is well to master. Since most teenagers live with their families or in dormitories where they share the use of the phone, certain basic courtesies should be recognized. For example, when you put through a call, ask at once for the person to whom you wish to speak, giving your name, in this way: "Hello, is Jane there please? This is Edith calling." When Jane comes to the phone repeat the salutation: "Hello, Jane. This is Edith." Then give the message you called to deliver. If Jane is not there or cannot come to the phone, you may leave a message for her if you keep it short and simple. Long, involved messages get twisted and are a nuisance to transmit. If you cannot get your message into a few words, leave word that you will call her back later or that you would like her to call you when she gets in. Thank the person to whom you have been talking, and hang up courteously.

Reserve your kidding and teasing for those who appreciate such fooling. Asking Jane's father if he knows who is calling is apt to get you in Dutch with Jane's family and to put Jane on the spot too. Nor is it wise to be too "cute" and full of nonsense with others of the family who may answer the phone. Keep your request and your message short and simple.

How to Answer a Phone

If you are expecting a call, it is well to be close by when it comes through. When the phone rings do not quickly take it for granted that it is your call; give the person on the other end of the line a chance to identify himself before you salute him. Picking up the receiver and saying, "Hi, sweetheart!" just may cause your dad's boss to sputter in consternation!

Your salutation starts best with your identification. You may simply repeat the number of your phone, immediately assuring the other party that the correct number has been connected. Or you can answer the phone by the formula, "Hello, this is the Gaynor residence." Another variation is to say, "Yes? This is John Gaynor speaking."

Should Girls Telephone Boys?

In a poll of high-school boys more than two-thirds said they do not like to have girls call them on the telephone. They feel that this is a boy's privilege, and that a girl seems forward when she phones a boy. They furthermore report that their families tease them about the girls who call them up at home.

Yet there may be times when a girl really must call a boy with an urgent message, to give him an invitation, or to make a request that cannot wait until she next sees him. When such a call is necessary, the girl must be unusually careful to observe the expected telephone courtesies. She should protect both the boy and herself from embarrassment by keeping her call short, and not telephoning him too often.

How to Hang up Politely

After the main business of the call has been transacted, some young people hang on to the phone, finding it hard to say good-bye and hang up. If this is caused by a little anxiety lest the other be offended by too abrupt a closing, a few simple formulas can be employed to end the call comfortably. If the other has called you, after the conversation seems completed you can say, "It was nice of you to call me. I'll see you soon." If you placed the call, you can conclude by saying, "I've enjoyed talking with you. Good-bye for now." If you feel it necessary, you can add, "I must run along now." Whatever your pet closing, it is courteous to hang up before unduly prolonging your telephoning.

Highway Habits

Q I just got my driver's license. How can I make my parents let me have their car occasionally?

A Better shift your point of view first. Ask for—not demand—the family car. Convince your parents of your driving ability. (Drive *them* somewhere, and show how capable you are!) Remind them that you'd like to repay rides from others. Drive a *logical* bargain—you'll find it will get you behind the wheel much faster than dramatics!

Don't drive a motor vehicle without an instruction permit or a driver's license. Your parents will be held liable for any accident or injury you cause while driving a motor vehicle. Employers must not permit a minor employee to drive a motor vehicle without a driver's license.

Whenever you are involved in an accident causing injury, death or damage, you must stop and give your name, address and registration number of your vehicle, and be prepared to show your driver's license.

Standard Highway Markings

Road signs and highway lines have been standardized throughout the country so that signs of the same shape always have the same general meaning. Familiarizing yourself with their shapes and meanings may save you serious trouble if rain or fog should obscure the lettering.

Double or multiple lines of the same color appearing in the center of the highway should not be crossed except when directed to do so.

Where the orange, yellow, or broken line appears on your side of the double center line, passing is permitted.

Be doubly careful where there are no highway markers or parallel lines, especially on rolling or winding roads. Extra caution is needed, too, in locating traffic signals and stop signs in a strange town. They may not conform to the placing of signs in your town.

Octagonal Signs mean STOP. You are approaching a stop street or dangerous corner.	*Round Signs mean RAILROAD CROSSING ahead. One horizontal bar means one track, two bars mean two tracks, etc.*	*Diamond-Shaped Signs mean SLOW DOWN. You are coming to a dangerous curve or hill, narrow bridge, end of pavement, bad road, or similar reason for cautious driving.*	*Square Signs usually give important information such as school zone, hospital zone, men working, etc.*	*Rectangular Signs usually give traffic directions, such as no left turn, keep to right, no parking, special speed limit, etc.*

23

HERBY HOTROCK
wasn't looking for more than one...

HERBY HOTROCK was the expert (he thought) driver who was away like a flash when the signal light turned green. And when he had to wait at a railroad crossing for a train to pass, he fumed and fretted until the last car came into sight. Then as it went by, Herby would whip across the tracks and be a block away before the other cars in the line began to move.

But Herby's speed was his undoing. You see, he never took into account that some crossings have two or more tracks. One day as he almost took the paint off a caboose getting across the first track, Herby plowed smack into the front of a locomotive of another train coming from the other direction on another track.

The folks around town miss Herby. At his funeral, however, the minister called attention to the error of Herby's ways. The gist of the minister's remarks was this: Don't rush across behind a passing train; there might be another one coming.

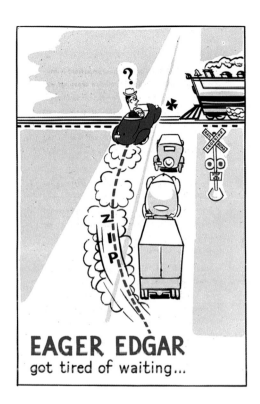

EAGER EDGAR
got tired of waiting...

EAGER EDGAR was one of those impatient fellows who thought waiting in line at railroad crossings was a terrific waste of his "valuable" time. He made a practice of pulling out of the line of waiting cars and speeding up the wrong side of the street to cross the tracks against the warning signal. Edgar had pulled this trick so many times he thought he couldn't miss.

Then one day he got the biggest (and last) surprise of his life. He and a locomotive arrived at the crossing at the same time. When a railroad crossing becomes a "disputed passage" between an automobile and a train, there is only one possible result . . . slow music for the motorist.

After the funeral, Eager Edgar's wife and two children had to move in with relatives. Now they go out to the cemetery each Sunday to put flowers on the grave of a man who was foolish enough to think he could win an argument with a locomotive.

Take our word for it, you can't win.

STOP-LOOK-LISTEN—AND LIVE!

Parties with Punch

Planning a Party?

Well, then, *do* plan it! Impromptu's are fine, but a real party gives you an opportunity to meet new acquaintances, make friends, and let your guests know one another better.

This may sound complicated, but the first few times you're entertaining give it a try.

CHECK family plans before you set a date. Even in a home of your own, you'll have to consider others.

PLAN to do most of the preparation. You'll need a little helping hand here and there, but your family won't be around to help you with a lifetime of entertaining.

INVITE your guests well ahead of time. Written invitations aren't necessary, but when phoning remember to give the date, hours of the party (and address to new acquaintances). Anything in the way of special clothing for sports such as skating or swimming should be mentioned, too.

KEEP the food simple! Don't spend all your time in the kitchen . . . there's a party on. And several overly expensive get-togethers just *may* take the place of that date dress or bathing suit you simply can't live without.

MAKE the menu, check the ingredients you'll need, and do the shopping a day or two ahead. Just be sure to have *plenty* of the things you serve.

Avoid Hostess Pains! Several days beforehand, plan the entertainment. See that records are selected, check the record player, collect ideas for games, or whatever's needed for evening fun. And while you're at it, inspect your dress. The successful hostess is dressed and waiting when her guests arrive.

Cut Down on Clean-Up for large groups, with paper plates, napkins and cups for informal gatherings. For a few, serve buffet style with the prettiest china . . . it's easy on you and mixes up the guests. But after the ball is over, just be sure to leave the kitchen clean and tidy!

Consider The Neighbors! Whether yours is a house or an apartment, remember that voices and music carry. In fairness to the baby who's *just* gotten to sleep. . . watch the noise.

Accidents Do Happen. If a family illness or crisis makes it impossible for you to have the party at home, first try having it at the home of a friend. Otherwise, just call your guests and explain you're postponing it. They'll understand.

P.S. *Next time you are a guest, remember your own party! The hostess has gone to a great deal of time and effort to make the evening enjoyable. Do your part by appearing at your most attractive and pleasant self.*

Being a Guest

Some people are always welcome wherever they go because
they know how to be good guests. Other persons find that
they are not so frequently invited out and that even when
they are guests, they do not enjoy it as much as they might.
These two things go together. If you are a good guest, you
are invited out and you do have a good time.

1. If hours have been stated, say eight to twelve, one adheres to the hours and leaves at twelve. (Informal gatherings break up earlier than a formal.)

2. You confine your play to the parts of the house that are indicated. You do not open doors or bureau drawers or go exploring into out-of-the-way places.

3. You keep your fun within bounds in regard to noise in order not to disturb others in the house or neighbors' houses beyond.

4. If you should be unfortunate enough to do any damage, making a ring on the table's surface by putting down a damp tumbler, spilling something on the floor, breaking a dish or the arm of a chair, you speak to your host or hostess at once and the very next day you set about making good the damage.

5. If you are drawing on the food supplies in the refrigerator you take only those indicated by your host or hostess. You do not, as a guest, do anything, or ask a young friend to do anything in his home, that is contrary to his custom. You don't ask to smoke or drink if your host does not offer smokes and drinks to you.

For Party Fun . . .

Other elections you may not win,
But this one thing we pray you'll heed,
An alcohol-free party will be voted
"Most likely to succeed."

Be gay, demure, and self-assured,
Free from false stimulation;
For whatever else is knowing,
Your personality is showing!

Beverage Ideas . . .

A simple syrup made by boiling one cup sugar in one cup water for three minutes may be kept in the refrigerator for sweetening any cold beverage.

For festive occasions, frost glasses by dipping the top rim of glass to a depth of 1/4 inch in water or lemon juice, then in granulated sugar. Chill glasses.

Freeze fruit juice cubes, such as grape, raspberry or loganberry juice in the ice cube tray of the refrigerator. These add color and flavor to lemonade or fruit drinks.

To make a soda—Place 2 or 3 tbsp. of your favorite syrup—chocolate, raspberry, etc., in a tall glass; add a scoop of ice cream. Fill glasses with ginger ale or carbonated water and stir briskly.

All sherbets served with ginger ale make a delicious punch. Other fruit juices may be added to the mixture if so desired.

Freeze ice cubes from colored fruit juices or cut cubes from frozen fruits; float in any punch or in a simple carbonated beverage such as ginger ale.

How to Ask a Girl for a Date

When a boy wants to ask a girl for a date, there are several rules to follow and pitfalls to avoid. First of all, he invites her specifically for a particular occasion, giving her the time, the place, and the nature of the affair. He says, for example, "May I take you to the game in Hometown Gym at two next Saturday afternoon?" Knowing all the relevant facts, she has a basis upon which to refuse or to accept. In the second place, he is friendly and acts as though he really wants her to accept his invitation. He looks at her with a smile while he waits for her reply. If she accepts, he seems pleased and arranges definitely for the time at which he will call for her. If she refuses, he says that he is sorry and suggests that perhaps another time she will go with him.

How Not to Ask Her

Boys find that girls do not like the indirect approach that starts, "What are you doing next Friday night?" That puts the girl "on a spot." Boys should not act as though they expect to be refused, as Amos does when he says, "I don't suppose you'd like to go on a date with me, would you?" This back-handed kind of invitation is apt to make the girl feel uncomfortable and is a mark of the boy's feeling of insecurity, too.

Girls do not like to be asked for dates at the last minute. It is no compliment to call a girl up the very evening of an affair. Even if she is free, she may be reluctant to accept such an eleventh-hour invitation. If circumstances have made it impossible to ask early for the date, then go right ahead, of course. Be frank about it. It sometimes happens that a girl has had no other invitation to an affair she wants very much to attend. Girls protest, too, that some boys try to date them for months ahead. Beth put her uncertainty about such an invitation this way: "Why sure, Mac, I'll go with you to the Prom next year if we both still think it's a good idea when the time comes."

Since asking a girl for a date is both a compliment and an invitation, a boy needs have no fear of using the simplest, most direct, and friendliest approach he can muster. He might be surprised to know how eager the girl has been to hear the words he is struggling to say!

To Remember

1. Never break a date, once made, unless a family crisis comes up.
2. Don't make a date feel uncomfortable by any word or action
   (a) You must not cause him to "lose face" in any manner or you will automatically forfeit his respect.
3. Keep conversation general—don't gossip or devote your attention to just one person if there are more than two of you involved.
4. Be quiet and considerate of others.
5. Apologize if you have over-reached yourself.
6. Never pet in public.

Ten Commandments of Good Conduct

1. Be a teen with taste, dressing appropriately for the occasion.
2. Act like a lady and he will treat you as such.
3. Be able to enjoy an everyday date as well as the glamour occasions.
4. Don't hang on him too possessively.
5. Don't have him fetch and carry just to create an impression.
6. Make up if you like but do not try to make over what you are.
7. Be popular with girls as well as boys.
8. Learn to like sports—it's an all-American topic in which boys are interested.
9. Don't be too self-sufficient; boys like to feel needed.
10. Be natural.

Boys' conduct on dates is a mirror image of girls' behavior. It takes two to make a good date. When the boy is suitably groomed and courteously at ease, he not only gives the girl a good time but he is likely to enjoy himself, too.

Both girls and boys must learn how to be smooth in their dating. None of us is born with the attributes of being a good date. All of us must learn how to conduct ourselves with poise and skill. Such learning can be fun, and it is important without question. On it hangs our feeling of being a successful member of one sex or the other.

Venereal Diseases

Two of the most common diseases are syphilis and gonorrhea. Although they are separate diseases, they are both contracted through sexual contact with an infected person. Both can become serious, but there is a cure for them. Infected persons should consult a private physician or a local health clinic.

It is impossible by looking at a person to know whether he has such a disease. The best protection is restricting sexual intercourse to marriage. Most states require a premarital examination of both bride and groom in order to determine the presence of venereal infection.

Syphilis

Syphilis is generally acquired through sexual intercourse with an infected person. However, it can be caught by an unborn baby from the mother. If the mother has been adequately treated during early pregnancy, the disease can be prevented from affecting the child.

In its primary stage, syphilis is characterized by a sore called chancre which usually appears on the genitals. Later there may be symptoms of sore throat, skin rash, and headaches.

In its more advanced stage, the symptoms may reappear as much as twenty years after the initial infection. The reason for this is that after the chancre disappears, the germs pass into the bloodstream where they remain quiescent.

Syphilis may attack any part of the body, including the heart and the nervous system. If concentrated in the brain, these germs may result in insanity and paralysis. This dread disease has also been known to leave disfiguring sores, blindness, and other incapacities. Detection of syphilis may be made by blood tests.

Gonorrhea

Gonorrhea is probably the most common of veneral diseases. Infection usually results from sexual intercourse with one who has the disease. Infection caused otherwise is not so common. It may be acquired in babies by means of a nurse or mother who already has the infection and who is not careful to wash her hands before caring for the infant.

Symptoms in the male are those of itching and burning at the opening of the penis. This is usually accompanied by a thick, yellowish discharge. These symptoms commonly appear about three days after exposure.

In the female, the symptoms are also that of burning and itching of the urethra. This is accompanied by a yellowish discharge. The symptoms may be more easily overlooked in a woman, but the aftereffects may become very serious.

Fortunately, these serious complications can usually be avoided by prompt and thorough treatment by competent medical doctors using effective medicines. The eyes of newborn babies are usually protected from possible gonorrheal infection of the mother by placing a solution in the baby's eyes at the time of birth.

Venereal infection is unlikely except in sexual intercourse with an infected person. Most localities have clinics where low-cost treatment is available, thereby affording a cure if cared for soon after infection. And yet it is unfortunate that although there are many facilities for handling veneral diseases, the incidence of such diseases is still significant.

Picnic Time Here?

Perhaps you're not the champion on the diving board or the golf course . . . but no one ever went wrong with a few specialties like these in the picnic hamper!

Forgetful? No chance of forgetting the salt or leaving plates back at the picnic grounds if you tape a small list of necessities inside the hamper. It's a good way to make sure you take everything you need and a handy way to check equipment when the picnic is over.

For refreshments on the trail, put crackers
together sandwich-style with cheese-spread
between; put them in a plastic freezer bag and
pin them onto your pack—or your hat! Carry an
apple or a tomato to eat with them.

Your Manners Are Showing

Are you the kind of girl who would dream up an elaborate and ridiculous plot to steal your girlfriend's boyfriend?

The compulsion comes to you one day during a geometry test after you have borrowed a pencil from him because something is wrong with your ballpoint pen. You flunk the test. His darling smile keeps coming between you and the angles. At the end of the period, you return the pencil. He hands it back.

"Keep it," he says with a smile. "You'll probably need it in your next class, and I have another."

Another smile! The light in his eyes! You tremble with excitement. This is it! He loves you, and you love him. No one, not even your dearest girlfriend must stand between you. After school you walk half a block behind him until both he and you are away from the crowds. Then you catch up and "just happen" to appear and join him. In a moment you "just happen" to stumble over nothing so that he must catch you in his arms.

He releases you quickly, a strange expression on his face, and then he strides ahead. You turn back toward your own home on the other side of town, overcome by the wonder of it all. You are sure the boy is too overcome by emotion to speak—that is why he went away so fast.

Unhappily, that evening you see him with your girlfriend. They are so engrossed in each other, neither sees you. Evidently the boy has spoken of your afternoon pursuit, however, for your girlfriend is cool toward you. In fact, you find yourself very lonely these days. You are a pitiful case because you are not only dishonest but ignorant.

The Social Climb

Marriage
Engagement
Courtship
Going Steady
Single Dating
Double Dating
Group Dating

THE SOCIAL CLIMB

Sex attraction

Psychic attraction

Sweetheart Love

Petting Defined

Petting is any combination of fondling, caressing, and kissing between members of the opposite sexes which tends to be sexually exciting to one or both of the partners. Some young people make a distinction between necking and petting. Sometimes they put it this way: Necking is any lovemaking above the neck—kissing, sitting or standing cheek to cheek, the lighter expressions of affection. Petting involves the caressing of other more sensitive parts of the body in a crescendo of sexual stimulation. The deep kiss or other erotically stimulating kissing and fondling are in the latter category.

Petting actually is the lovemaking that precedes and makes the couple ready for full sex intercourse. In marriage this same thing is called foreplay, because it comes before and prepares the couple for coitus. Thus in marriage, petting has a very real role in getting the woman ready to receive her sex partner in the fullest sense. Before marriage, petting stimulates both male and female in the same way, without offering them the final step in consummation. What to do about petting, therefore, is a challenge to all young unmarried people today. They must answer for themselves: 1) how far they mean to go; 2) how they can tell where to stop; 3) how to stop; and 4) just what petting means to each of them.

The Urge to Pet

It is normal to want to be near the person you like. This is true even in the most casual gathering. You enter a room, your eyes scan the people already there for a friendly face, an inviting glance. You go at once to be near the people you like and in whose friendliness you feel secure. When you are free to choose whom you will sit by, you seek out the one you like to be with. As significant things are said or common experiences recalled, you look at each other in a personal way, you touch the other's hand, you seek contact with the person who means something to you. When you like a person, you want to be close to him or her. You enjoy physical contact with those you like. This is true not only between members of opposite sexes but also of persons in the same sex group.

Sam was talking with a bunch of fellows after school one day when he felt an arm thrown over his shoulder from behind. He turned and recognized his pal Jeff. Without halting the story he was telling, he grinned at Jeff and pulled him into the circle. It was all so natural that neither of them realized how differently Sam might have responded if that arm over his shoulder had belonged to some person he did not like! We take it for granted that friends will seek and enjoy contact with each other.

When those friends are of different sexes, a peculiarly pleasant quality is added. A girl thrills to just being close to a boy she likes very much. A boy goes out of his way to walk with, talk with, look at, listen to, touch, and be touched by the girl who especially appeals to him. Little gestures that indicate that the other is enjoying being near can be exquisitely enjoyable.

Such a couple soon find their hands seeking each other as they sit together in a movie or walk down a path. Hand-holding brings both a warm sense of response that tends to continue. From then on the friendly kiss, the deeper lovers' kiss, the urge to hold the other close, to fondle and caress, come as normally as breathing. The attraction of members of one sex to the other is strangely compelling, urgently insistent, and all too little understood in these days when so much freedom of expression is possible.

Petting as a Game

Some irresponsible young people play at lovemaking as a kind of game. There are boys and men who deliberately get girls into petting situations just to see how far they can go. Such males take advantage of the unwary and are always a challenge to any woman, however sophisticated. Adolph bragged around school about the number of girls he had "had." He rarely went back to the same girl twice, but rather played a game of seeing how many girls he could seduce with his love act.

Some unscrupulous girls will lead boys and men on in just the same way. Such girls do not and cannot really love the men they go out with. They are exploiting men for the sense of power they may gain over them. Such love-pirates only play a kind of risky game, with none of love's richness, none of its real satisfaction, none of its beauty and permanence. Being seduced by such a person is no compliment and should be no temptation to the young person who knows the difference between expressing deep affection and using the other sex for temporary and very superficial gratification.

The Process of Petting

Whether in an exploitive situation, as just described, or between mutually devoted couples who express in their lovemaking the deepest concerns for each other's welfare, petting is a process of physical involvement between members of the opposite sex which follows patterns that can be predicted. One step leads to the next in a way that can be reliably anticipated.

The various steps in the process can be identified as they move toward goals that are recognizable. Let us analyze more closely these characteristics of petting.

48

Lovemaking Tends to Be Habit-Forming

We learn to love and be loved first of all in our families. These earliest learnings are elaborated and developed as we mature and have warm contacts with beloved friends. Here, too, the habit-forming elements continue. The boy who has learned to hold his girl's hand as he walks down the street with her will tend to do so habitually. The girl and boy who say good-night with a kiss tend to expect it, to feel deprived if they do not have it, and to come together in that kiss spontaneously, almost without thinking.

In much the same way, persons who have learned to pet when with an attractive person of the other sex soon develop the habit of petting to the point where it is extremely difficult not to. They tend to expect and to demand the level of expression to which they are accustomed, and only with willpower and conscious control are they able to stop short of that point.

Fred and Nan had developed the habit of petting to the place where they could enjoy little else. All through the early parts of the evening, each was preoccupied with thoughts of what would happen when the finally got off alone. Everything else faded out, and only their petting seemed important. Finally their relationship became so focused on petting, and petting alone, that they decided to break up and not see each other so much. The first girls that Fred dated after he and Nan stopped going steady had quite a time with him. For he tried to pet them in the same way that he and Nan had done over the months. It wasn't because he cared specially for them, but rather that he had developed the petting habit to the place where any girl was a stimulus to the routine.

The sex urge is universal. Its satisfaction is learned. We learn to satisfy our feelings of attraction and response to others in many different ways, depending upon who we are, where we live, and what we expect of ourselves. It is something like our satisfaction of hunger. We all feel hungry at times. But the way we eat, and what, and with whom, and how often, and how we feel about it, differ enormously from one person to the next, as well as from one culture to another. So it is with sex satisfaction. The sex urge is native and universal. Sex satisfaction is learned and highly individualized.

49

Sex Tends to Focus on the Person

Just as Fred and Nan found that each brought forth in the other the urge to pet, so sex expressions tend to focus on the individual with whom there has been some previous satisfaction. Most of us know very attractive people of the other sex with whom we would not think of being intimate. C. K. always kissed Caroline when he saw her, not because Caroline wanted him to, or even because he found her particularly kissable! The simple reason was that soon after they met, they were together at the wedding of a mutual friend where everyone was kissing everyone else. He kissed her then and has continued the habit ever since.

When we realize that the relationship between the sexes finds its greatest meaning and satisfactions when it is based upon mutual affection, mutual respect, and a real love for each other as whole personalities, then we can see that becoming just a sex object in the other's eyes can warp the whole relationship. Sex is always there. It lies close to the surface in all male-female relationships. It can always be called forth to intensify a relationship between the sexes. But as soon as sex is given free expression, the relationship tends to fixate on a sexual level, except, of course, after marriage when all of life is encompassed in the fullness of the relationship.

Sex Play Builds to Climax

Any physical intimacy between the members of opposite sexes tends to lead to the next step in the sequence of lovemaking that leads to the climax of complete release. Left uncontrolled, the urgencies of stimulation rush a couple through stage after stage of their involvement until nature has satisfied herself in intercourse. These forces are often very strong and insistent. Once released, they tend to press for completion. So it is a wise couple, an intelligent young person, who knows where to stop and how.

Physical Signs

When the expression of affection begins to be sexually exciting, certain physical signs appear which can be detected by one or both members of the couple. Because of differences between boys and girls in the way they are made and the ways in which they have been brought up, the boy usually experiences the first symptoms of sexual expression. His face may become flushed. Usually his breathing becomes rapid, his pulse is fast, and his heart starts to pound. Changes in his sex organs are obvious. The girl as well as the boy may find that hands perspire freely under sexual stimulation. Some girls experience an all-over relaxation. The alert couple can detect other physical signs of arousal of sex feelings that should operate as caution signals for them.

Compulsion to Continue

When either or both feel urgently impelled to continue, it is a sign that sexual stimulation is already present. Nature causes us to respond in a spiraling crescendo of feeling that is easier to stop in its early stages than it is near the peak of excitability. The couple who really love each other enough to protect themselves and their relationships from ill-advised behavior guard against getting so involved that there is a compulsion to continue. Likewise the individual girl or boy, caught in a petting situation with a person who wants only that, can recognize the first hint of urgency as a stop sign.

Your Own Feeling of Rightness and Wrongness

You can gauge where to stop by how you feel after various kinds of dates. If you feel embarrassed about what you did on last night's date when you wake up in the morning, you probably overstepped your own sense of what is right. If you find it hard to look in each other's eyes when you next meet, then apparently you both feel that what you have done was not quite as it should have been. But if you awaken after a date with a feeling of happiness and joy of living, if you find yourself eagerly looking forward to seeing your date again, if you like being together, working together, sharing all sorts of things with each other, then it probably means that your physical love-making is not out of hand.

The Girl's Responsibility

Down through the ages it has been considered the female's responsibility to keep relationships between the sexes under control The big reason apparently is that women are less easily excited by sex stimulation and more slowly moved to demand sexual contact. It is true that on the whole girls are more slowly aroused and can stop lovemaking more easily than the average male can. The female's response is an all-over one, generalized rather than localized, and more gradual in its buildup than that of the typical male.

Coupled with this physiologic difference is the fact that girls and boys alike, as well as almost everyone else, consider it the girl's responsibility "to keep the boys in line." If two lovers are swept off their feet, it is the girl that is blamed. She is held responsible. She should have known better.

Getting a boy to stop his lovemaking is hard for some girls. They are so hungry for loving that they cling to any expression of affection that they can evoke. Girls may be so afraid of losing the boy's attention that they dare not refuse him intimacies that he seems to enjoy. Some girls just do not know how to say "No" to a boy without hurting his feelings or offending something fine in their relationship. Yet a girl can keep the expressions of affection between herself and her boyfriend on a comfortable basis without losing his love, or his friendship, or the sense of everything's being all right between them.

Stopping lovemaking that is already advancing at a rapid rate is not easy. But it can be done. Cora was snuggling close to her favorite boyfriend in the car late one night. They were both relaxed and happy. They were very fond of each other. He began to kiss her, and she responded eagerly. Then something new came into their lovemaking as his hand slipped down between her breasts and his kiss took on an intensity that was frightening. Cora struggled free of his embrace, shook her curls with a jerky little laugh, saying, "Ooooh, please, you are too much for me."

The Boy's Responsibility

Boys, too, have a responsibility for controls in their relationships with girls. A boy who takes a girl out without the supervision and the chaperonage that once prevailed is duty-bound to see to it that he returns her to her home unharmed. Furthermore, he is jointly responsible with her for the quality and the nature of their relationship. It is as much his duty as hers to keep their friendship on a basis that both can continue to enjoy without endangering themselves or those they hold dear.

We know that boys are usually aware of sexually stimulating situations before the average girl may sense what is happening. Boys sometimes are baffled by the things nice girls do that are sexually exciting, without realizing that oftentimes the girl has no idea of how provocative her behavior may be. The boy in such a position gently eases them both into a more comfortable position without taking advantage of her innocent seduction. Sometimes it becomes necessary for a boy to instruct his girlfriend on some of the facts of life.

Fritz and Jane were very fond of each other. They had been going together steadily for some time, when Fritz found it necessary to talk things over with her. He said something like this: "I love you very much, so much that I want you close to me always. But when you sit on my lap like this, my feelings become almost more than I can cope with. So slide over on your own side of the seat and let's go get a hamburger." Fritz was taking his share of the responsibility for their relationship.